Unaccountable Weather

Poems by

KATHRYN KIRKPATRICK

Press 53
Winston-Salem

Press 53
PO Box 30314
Winston-Salem, NC 27130

First Edition

A TOM LOMBARDO POETRY SELECTION

Cover design by Kevin Morgan Watson

Cover art, "Ayanami" Copyright © 2011 by Carlo d'Anna

Author photo by Frederica Georgia

Printed on acid-free paper

ISBN 978-1-935708-37-7

UNACCOUNTABLE WEATHER

For William,
David, and the whole village.

And in memory of Beamish and Ceilidh
who stayed until the work was done.

The wisewomen say you must live in your skin, call it home,
no matter how battered or broken, misused by the world, you can heal.

Paula Meehan

Acknowledgments

My thanks to the editors, readers, and staff of the following journals where these poems first appeared, sometimes in other versions:

Calyx: "The Garden of Lost Breasts" & "Maria Makes Out"; *Cave Wall*: "Threshold" & "Struck"; *Cortland Review*: "The Poem I Didn't Write"; *Ekphrasis*: "Bird Goddess" & "Aphrodite"; *Hawk & Handsaw*: "Alter"; *The Healing Muse*: "Physical Therapy"; *Kakalak*: "Lynn Makes Love"; *Natural Bridge*: "Diana"; *Poem*: "For the Mother Who Brought Me Birdseed" & "Rewriting Class Mobility"; *PoemMemoirStory*: "Radiation Treatments"; *Salamander*: "Coming Back"; *Shenandoah*: "After the Cave Paintings"; *The South Carolina Review*: "Chemotherapy" & "Dehydration"; *storySouth*: "synesthesia after anesthesia" & "Every Small Death"; *2River View*: "Artemis"; *Syracuse Cultural Workers' Women Artists Datebook*: "Glenda in the Garden"

"Lynn Makes Love" was chosen by Colette Inez for second place in the 2008 *Kakalak* Poetry Contest.

"Threshold" appeared on *Verse Daily* on March 17, 2009.

"Bird Goddess" was a finalist in the 2006 *Ekphrasis* poetry contest.

I am grateful to the many readers of this manuscript for their help and encouragement, especially William Atkinson, Natalie Anderson, Ed Madden, Robert Hill, Susan Ludvigson, and Sharon Sharp. Tom Lombardo, poetry editor at Press53, has given these poems invaluable attention and care.

Half of all author proceeds from this book will support research on cancer prevention.

Contents

3 THRESHOLD

4 SANCTUARY ON THE MOUNTAIN

Introduction
by Tom Lombardo

A collection that begins with this line...

Once we even used bacon grease—

...is one that gets your attention quickly.

And once you realize in the second poem that the narrator "feels like [it's] the end of the world...with the unwelcome bloom in my breast," that this collection tells the story of the diagnosis, treatment, and recovery from breast cancer, you go back to read that first poem, and its final lines take your breath away.

> ...my body, that last teacher
> to draw me up short, saying
> *here you are now,*
> *the weight of a particular past*
> *squarely on your chest.*

The shock of diagnosis gives way to a poet's wondering why and how and when.

Poet Kathryn Kirkpatrick takes her readers through the entire course. There is the clinical reality that begins with

> what you never
> imagined you'd ever need to hear:
> *it's time to save your life.*

There is the kindness of strangers, like the woman whose son is in chemo who befriends the narrator, and the lover who gently touches her scars as an act of foreplay. Ms. Kirkpatrick has also found humor in the struggle in the stories of others, like Glenda, who works topless and breastless in her garden even when the neighbors call the cops on her, and Donna, who gets so excited flat-foot dancing that she takes out her Dolly Parton prostheses and flings them at her surprised partner.

Through the course of this collection, Ms. Kirkpatrick works brilliantly with the symbols of feminine personae from antiquity that create metaphors for a modern feminine persona that many women become in their struggles to live and love their daily lives through illness. Ms. Kirkpatrick begins by invoking Athena as her anthem:

> …
> The flames at her chest tell us
> what she has suffered,
> what she has made of her suffering.

Athena and her sister-goddesses lead us through this collection.

> …
> one day we are all called back
> to mortal bodies, the unimaginable
> before us like the raised root on the path
> we didn't see, and we are down in it,
> all that muck and grime

In the muck and grime, we find success and hope—small and large—and recovery. Throughout *Unaccountable Weather*, the poet's stance and tone remain straight ahead, objective. There is no sentimentality in this dance between life and death.

… she does not ask to be rescued…

> She does not avoid
> inevitable pain,
> but asks:
> what need not be suffered?

Tom Lombardo
Poetry Series Editor

1

Every Small Death

Called Back

Once we even used bacon grease—
nothing else under the sun
to turn us so golden, though fat
on flesh was near the bone
enough, our own slim bodies
bait we were learning could lure
more than we'd bargained for—

men twice our age, for example,
who reached for our breasts.
Almost ripe, one said
as before I knew it
he had mine in hand,
a chill in the dim hallway,
my sunburn pricking.

Born after the bomb,
we had no conception
of life without plastic and pesticides
though sometimes we dreamed,
unaccountably, of backroads
and blackberry briers,
our hands in unspoiled soil,
pulling radishes, carrots, and beets.

Mostly we strode free,
burnished and blistered,
hop-scotching cities and towns,
rootless in rental houses,
Chevrolets nosing us beyond limits,

TV ads blaring *better* and *more,*
one suburb much like another,
convenient as Kmart and cul-de-sacs,
without fields or cows or canning,
until our bodies called us back.

That summer after father died
sun on my chest left its heat
like the rage that hid my grief.
I lay burnt up and lost
in my bedroom, slamming
doors, testing the primal scream,
no wise woman sitting me down
and braiding my hair,
just heat and burn
heat and burn
my body, that last teacher
to draw me up short, saying
here you are now,
the weight of a particular past
squarely on your chest.

Every Small Death

Mid-winter the daylilies crown.
Moss phlox open lavender spokes.
Months early, daffodils spike.
Peonies risk their ruby wrists

as the confounded seasons
fool everything not wary
of the still-measured light.
A young man behind the counter

in town says it feels like the end
of the world, and I nod, me
with the unwelcome bloom in my breast.
It is winter, *so dormant, so die*

I say to the chaos of green
on my hill, to my body's unruly
cells. We will stand it, both of us,
the mountain and me.

We will relearn every small death.

Department of Mammography,
Because I Want To Live

The room is cold.
I stand in my shift like a beggar.

Glass plates clamp each breast—
no tenderness, just urgency to *see*,

see, see–tissue yielding its secrets,
illuminated breasts on light boxes,

open book for the radiologist to read.
Wizard of Oz, he's calling the shots

from behind closed doors,
magnification, new angle

and whatever courage and heart
I might need seem lost

in the tangle of *stand very still,
do that again, hold your breath.*

I tango with the machine, lean away
from my captured breast, hand on metal.

The dance is hours long.
I wait while others take a turn.

The room is always cold
where I stand in my shift like a beggar.

Athena

Not wooed by the snake like Eve
but one with the snake like Medusa.

This is wisdom with bite,
appraisal cool and round as an egg.

Forget the olive tree, flute,
yoked oxen, and bridled horse.

Forget Prometheus who tried to take credit.

The flames at her chest tell us
what she has suffered,
what she has made of her suffering.

Western Medicine

After so many years let go,
set free, the doctor's door
at my back, blood pressure normal,
cholesterol fine, mole benign,
I am finally called back,
no slipping out to the warm afternoon,
that welcome slant of light.

A friend says *I can't possibly imagine*
but one day we are all called back
to mortal bodies, the unimaginable
before us like the raised root on the path
we didn't see, and we are down in it,
all that muck and grime

until these others appear—
wood-sprite in the white coat,
green man in scrubs,
radiation goddess with her resident—
who have always lived here
in the half light, staking a claim
to the long life, the full allotment

of years, saying now what you never
imagined you'd ever need to hear:
it's time to save your life.

What's Stayed With Me

When Charlton Heston fell to his knees
beside the half-buried Statue of Liberty
in *Planet of the Apes*, I was a kid
in the backseat of a Chevrolet
out with my family at the drive-in.

Who knows what my parents thought,
adult and distant, in the front seat.
It was summer and Saturday night,
far from homework and chores and the bills
my father paid beside his coffee cup.

We were parked and tethered to our post,
the sound box a welcome familiar
on the car door, the big screen promising
more than we'd ever have, popcorn
and Pepsi nirvana enough for one evening.

Missiles and coups and DDT
were nightmares I hadn't yet dreamed.
Who knows what I thought, elbows
hooked over the front seat, adolescence
ahead like the war zones up on the screen.

What's stayed with me is the image
of everything lost, the land defiled,
liberties half-buried, an ordinary man
like my father, sunk and stranded, beside
the other side of the American dream.

The Garden of Lost Breasts

At first they are lonely,
severed from the capable chest.
Without feet, without bodies to carry them,

they arrive on the backs of herons,
in the pouches of possums.
Because they have often fed others,

the animals refuse to eat them,
will not leave them in labs
on pathology slides.

Instead they bring them here
like racehorses put out to pasture.
Having done the work

of nurture and beauty, nothing
more is required of these breasts—
coffee or golden, ivory or pink,

they have all forgiven someone.
Now they lounge under willows
or sun themselves by the lake.

And here among so many others,
they soon forget the lover's tongue,
the low-cut gown, the matching breast.

Artemis

She knows better. She always has.
Icicle at the eye. No tears.

Behind her the bare branches of winter.
A crescent moon.

But the coldness is not, has never been,
brittle. Beneath the sheen of ice,
she is bear-hearted, lynx-limbed.

What woman would not trust herself
to this? Not safe haven exactly. Rather,
a welcome danger.

The Poem I Didn't Write

came on me in daylight
where they dress deer
for burger or roast.

I didn't want to write
about the doe
legs stiff in the air

and the young boy
camouflaged to the hilt
checking out her privates.

I wanted no part
of what flooded me
like memory, my own body

unconscious, splayed for
the catheter before surgery.
But here it is,

a protest gaining strength,
the poem like a sit-in,
like a print job in a queue

refusing other poems,
desiring the body's dignity,
even in the dismemberings.

synesthesia after anesthesia

waking up like a needle
in a haystack
afraid to be found

and if found
to make nothing more
than a stitch in water

but even so
the unimaginable ripple
might touch the tongue

of a passing doe
who has bent to drink
so long and so deeply

I sound my fear
and swim the current
in her liquid eye

2

Finding the Heart

Rite of Passage

That spring our neighbor stood naked
behind his screen door,
his body a quiet threat
in the row of rental houses

so I took to the sidewalk, stopped
cutting across his backyard.
I wanted my own body to bloom
and I painted my lips behind the bushes,

rolled up the elastic waist of my skirt,
held hands with the new boy from Puerto Rico.
I was ready for love
though I couldn't find my vagina,

the tampon diagrams a puzzle of passages
I didn't yet know how to travel.
My parents discussed me behind closed doors
while I listened to the song of my body,

but there was no Maypole celebration,
no rituals of maidenhood,
flowers in my hair like Botticelli's
round, dancing girls.

Instead, I was seen on the street arm in arm,
and came home to each dress torn from my closet,
my father ripping across seams, my mother's labor
lost, our hours over patterns and fabric

blown petals at my feet.
I turned to jeans and flannel shirts,
the undesirable indestructible,
my longing a pulse turned furtive.

Post-op Pop

When I woke up in recovery,
I had this song in my head.

I've got you under my skin.
I've got you deep in the heart of me.

Frank Sinatra wasn't who I'd expected
after losing my breast.

But all that night in the medical
twilight, he kept singing,

so deep in my heart
that you're really a part of me

The part of me that chose the song
wouldn't switch it off or change it,

persistent broken record, insistent wooer.
I'd doze and wake. Nurses. IV.

I tried so hard to resist.
I said to myself this affair

it never will go so well.
Strange how I wondered

what it meant, the song opaque
as the surgical bra I couldn't look into.

18

Astarte

Crowned by a crescent moon
or the horns of a cow,
she can go either way.

Will it be the easy conflagration,
Mars as the goddess of war?
Or a choice more hard-won,
love, the offered cup?

Perhaps, like her, you're beyond oppositions:
let a flying fish split the forehead,
a chalice cradle the setting sun.

But let's not be entirely opaque.
When you see her dressed in scarlet,
one eye veiled, you know
the darkness behind her
is a necessary darkness,
makes the light possible.

And the terror? You know too
she is merciless as a lidless eye.
And must choose each moment
not to be.

Barb's Bag

Tethered to an IV, alone,
full bladder strange
after anesthesia, plastic tubes

in my side, my chest, draining
to bulbs the surgeon calls grenades,
an image more apt than welcome.

Skin on muscle, skin on bone.
And I've only two safety pins
and a floppy, gray gown,

so that the hospital bed to the bathroom door
seems immeasurably far and I can't
make my way, when I see spilling

from my luggage, the woven bag
you gave as a gift one birthday,
rich rusts and reds, a long cord,

and though you're gone from this life,
I inch toward what you've left me,
the cord soon circling my neck,

the filling bulbs in the purse's pouch,
and once again, even from this distance,
you give me exactly what I need.

Maria Makes Out

If you want to see them, you can.
I had the reconstruction. They cut

muscle like two small footballs
from my back. That's what they put

in my chest. I said, Look, I'm not getting
much out of this. At least make them bigger!

It was three weeks in bed, tubes
waving their octopus arms,

pain jiggering me so much worse
than when they took my breasts.

But I woke up, put my hands
on my chest, and oh my, I felt like

a woman again. When I showed them
to Rita in the parking lot, my boss got

an eyeful too. I don't care. I couldn't
be happier. I might have done different

if Ramon hadn't left, but I need
to make love again. Who would want

me like that? If you decide to get some,
I'd be happy to show you mine,

just so you know what to expect.
Next surgery I'm getting nipples.

Finding the Heart

Under the hydrangea, a heart
the dogs have found, a deer's
left by a hunter in our woods,
the carcass gutted where it lay, and I,
having never seen anything
like it, larger than anyone's fist
I know of, fetch the shovel because
it is so newly out of the body,
I am sure it was beating
only yesterday or the day before
and so bare beside the knife's
fresh cut and so powerful, somehow,
as if it did the work of living
still that I cannot bear
this awful cleaving from
the breath it made
and I dig a small grave.

Eurydice

The blindfold is apt,
                    but she can see:
there is always more than one answer.

Crows nest in her hair. Her face reappears
in each shadow.

She does not ask to be rescued,
                    but Orpheus arrives
in a sandstorm, intending heroics.

Bent on his own story,
                  no wonder
he looks back
        not for her
but for what they will say
of him.
        Had he really wished to see

her earth brown skin,
the full moon of her eyes,

he needn't have traveled so far.

Chemotherapy

Up from the massage table
I catch sight of myself
in the unavoidable mirror.

Afternoon light doesn't blink.
Basic bald head. Bare pudendum.
Soft pile of belly and hips.

Once mirrors drew me like friends,
broke my gloomy moods
with a smile, eyes brighter

than I'd remembered. Now I'm *sacra*
to myself, a neutral suggestion,
transpersonal form. Stripped

to Neolithic goddess, I'm all
that's behind all that will ever be,
prima mater, prima material,

impersonal as rain, kneaded
to dozens of shapes, except
that my chest is scarred

which is what you'd expect
of a goddess in this 21st century.

Dehydration

Not just me braving another needle before dawn,
but also that other, sinuous and sleek, my selkie self,
so that for the moment I am only a sheath of human body,
and, yes, one step aside from the hospital room,
where they perform the kindness of saving my life,
I am deep in the current, undulating torso, flippers

tireless as the oars I need to take me back to shore
where I slide again toward my human skin which waits
on this foreign bed made familiar, accompanied and calm,
because she swims seaweed and salt.

For the Mother Who Brought Me Birdseed

When the finches find the webbed bags of seed,
will any kernel of Nyger contain
the mother, her sleeping son on one side,
me on the other, and all that remains
of his IV, of mine, binding us both
to the future tense, *to live, we will live*

like the finches feeding, yellow fits of life,
outside the window at the clinic
where we roost in recliners, hooked up to
pre-meds, infusions, quietly coaxing
our lives back to our outstretched palms, as you
would, too, as without a word, but listening,
this mother, her son's treatment done, has heard
me say I want seed to feed the birds.

Diana

Not to let the child die
is her charge.

She holds the bow before
her bare belly,

unstrung for the moment,
                          at dusk.
An arrow is not
the only protection.

And birth is not always
lava between the thighs.

The mouth of the child is her open throat.
The eye of the child is the unharmed doe.
The heart of the child is the dropped shield.
The foot of the child is her pointing toe.

3

Threshold

After the April Freeze

The Japanese maple leafs again,
but this time mid-trunk,
as if none of its limbs
can be trusted. Rather,
a cautious, covert showing
as when a risk has been taken
and regretted, the price disastrously high.

So here are the blood-red shoots
at the middle of a still-hardy life.
Awkward and vulnerable, they pelt
the tree's slender core.
Going to the heart of the matter,
ugly and necessary, they have
no time for the pleasures of the human eye.
This is the urgent business of survival.

The tree lives its compromised beauty,
up the chakras, registering how it once trusted—
oh, that was its only sin, to trust—

the delirium of seasons,
earth's spiking fever, false spring.

Glenda in the Garden

Bare-chested isn't bare-breasted,
whatever the police might say.
After I lost both of mine
to the cancer, I started working
topless in the yard. *Bilateral*
mastectomy the doctors called it,
but those words smell like alcohol.
Might as well have been doves
roosting on my chest. Now they've flown,
and I take mourning into the open air
where the weeping cherry is losing
another limb to the tent worms.
It's okay—the tree will survive, gnarled
beauty more a comfort to me now
than any straining perfection.

When I read about pesticides,
how they madden a living cell,
I stopped spraying the roses.
I turn compost in the wire bin,
and my body feels clean, the sun
like a lover's hands, the scars
on my chest healed into another
landscape. Out here, in just my capris,
I feel a peace I can't find indoors.
So when the police arrive again,
I smile and offer tea.
Indecent exposure they claim,
but those words taste like metal.
There aren't laws for bodies like mine.

Physical Therapy

She massages the scar,
small circles with an index finger
on my chest's red line.

What once was private and sexual
is now in the public domain,
though there's intimacy still

in the vulnerable altered
body, so that hours after
the scar's been touched, I

sit beside myself in a public
space, diffused, remapping
my flesh, lost breast visible

in my shirt's different drape,
skin healing over bone, arm
rehinging, a stranger's face registering

my half-inch hair, *what manner
of being?* until sunlight finds its way
through the latticed glass panes—

I am here.

Alter

Are you a man or a woman? She's squinting
at my inch long hair, the flat side of my chest,
and what are the answers for the state

I'm in? Yes or no? Him or her?
I'm way beyond that roadblock, carried
like a hawk on funneling air

to the Land of the Sick, through the Land
of the Dead, what I was before
not immaterial, but materially remade.

Yet here at the afternoon bus-stop,
sixty days into a drought, the landscape
stoic with thirst, I keep to the facts

*I'm a woman who's been through
chemotherapy* which accounts at least
for appearances if not for the stunned

edge where all these months I've lived,
another voice sounding my body's currents,
the earth's mantle opened and shut,

a compass in my chest conversing
with cloud and branch and blade.
Now a man with a plastic tank on his back

aims his wand at tufts of grass. *Pesticides?*
I bristle, and he nods while I step onto
the curb, away from the world that made me,
toward the same world where I am remade.

Bird Goddess

Because she is ancient
and winged, her whole body
perched and dappled, legs
fading into the trunk of a tree

who will understand her?

She could as easily rise
toward the daunted sky
as send roots into the willing earth.

Who will value such scope,
such ambiguity, however fertile?

She must be woman or bird or tree.
She cannot be all three.

Torso slim against a giant moon,
wingtips arcing the sun's yolk,

she is pure possibility
at that moment before
category.

Clearance

Catalogues in my mailbox
are messages from another world.

Star Dream Bag. Sanctified Earring.
Blue Tropics Confidence Shirt.

Who buys this stuff now that we know
imported means half-starved, half-poisoned,

outside our borders, outside our ken?
I hunker down like in high school,

the other girls daily in Casual Corner
and Belk, me in my jeans, on my bike,

making the best of what I couldn't afford,
not knowing, then, as I turned my thin

rebellious back, that necessity made
the best choice, and going without

was staying within
a common human limit.

Unaccountable Weather

Easter snow and four nights the thermometer
dips.
      Blueberry blossoms hold for a while
but this is serious cold after weeks of early spring.

Hostas melt by the drive.
                  Rosebushes burn to the ground.

The head-turning warmth had lulled us,
                  each in our own way,
the mock orange cautious, the lilac rash.

Who doesn't ache for perpetual spring,
lives beyond illness and blight?

Only the rose of sharon doubted, the trumpet vine held
her tongue.
      Come back I whisper to the plum trees,
to the pear, to myself.
              Come back through the scorch
and blister of frost.
              Try again the warmer air, the sunlight
and rain.
            We have lost a season of blossom and fruit,
but see how the lilac grows back from the ground, spirea
nudge past false starts.

Though we're tried to death
              by unaccountable weather,
trust that this is really spring.

Aphrodite

Of course light unfurls from her body,
and the moon glows gold in the distance.

But why does her face float alone in its wings
of turquoise and umber and labia mauve?

No apple breasts. No belly. Nothing of what
we know of her luscious thighs.

Instead we are given the brain, its veined
complications. A serene expression, slightly sad.

Passion has burnished her just beyond heartbreak.
Who are the two in the breast of the dove?

When she opens the spiral of her third eye,
she is not entirely alone.

Neither is she wholly accompanied.

Lynn Makes Love

Of course I meant to tell him.
I waited for the right moment
like a farmer waits for rain.

But how do you tell a man
you want for a lover
you have only one breast?

For years before I met him
I wore that prosthesis like armor,
no more sloppy stares at my chest,

no eyes of a stranger half-mast
then back to my face, full
of the difference. Okay, it's the missed

step on the stair for a while. It's
a new kind of balance. But muscadines
and butternut squash still taste sweet.

So when John reached for me that night,
we were both on the brink of knowing
who we might be, his breath fast

at my neck, our urgent pushing up
of my skirt, and then the sweet thrust
let fly that weighted rubber breast

over our heads and across the room.
For a moment I was only my heart's
staccato, pleasure the same beat

as fear. I suppose there might have been
tears. But I remember the laughter,
on and on, both of us at once.

Later when we made love again,
I took off my clothes. He put his hand
on the smooth, un-nippled plane
of my chest, and I came home.

Threshold

The jagged trail of pee
starts on the porch mat's
rough weave, crosses
the foyer into the front room
and ends on the rug
brought from Turkey.
What can she mean?
My dear oldest dog, trained
these twelve years to outside
and inside, has always been
clear about rules, no shredded
books in her history, not
a single mangled shoe.
But here she's let flow
behind my waking
back, speaking her language
of potent scent and boundary
on this day of all days
when I'm to be measured
and charted, the distance
from heart to lung
calibrated, from lymph node
to rib, the threshold of my
body crossed and re-crossed
so radiation can scour my cells.
Ceilidh knows the boundaries
have changed. She sleeps by
my bed and we breathe
through each other's dreams.
Perhaps because I've made
no offering to the gods

done no threshold ritual
of my own, she is marking
the moment. *Mop all you want*
she seems to say as I run
for the bucket and sponge.
Now this world is in you
and you are in this world.

Radiation Treatments

for John

No wonder he won't stay put.
All day gray gowns unfurl
to the chest's red seam or the thigh's

saying *who does not perish*
saying *give us more time*
as he lines up tattoo and table

so photons, so electrons can dance
that maddening paradox, mend
while unmending. We chat

music and gardens, weather
and roads, until he darts behind
closed doors, leaves me

to the machine's stark whine.
It's how he travels the country,
gypsies west then south, no town

untainted, no field, no stream.
Out west they bring their RVs
to do chemotherapy.

It's how he travels this life, daily
reminder our days are numbered.
Don't look back he tells me

as he holds out his hand
this technician, technically not
lover or friend. But how many times

light-footed, on his way to somewhere
else, does he gentle my body
beneath the staring plates,

cast out the demons
as I reach back for the metal rail,
see the damage, the scar

still calling me by my name.

4

Sanctuary on the Mountain

Rewriting Class Mobility

Instead of the empty room
which stays empty when you arrive,

your college bags dropped at your feet,
the light off, you standing alone

long enough, since they know you are here,
to see that making good

will not be made much of,
instead of that miserable story

dragging you around like an old shoe,
here's your mother with your favorite cake,

your brother has hung a banner,
and rather than a power tool

droning on and on, a hushed delight
greets you as your father steps out

from behind his scowl, turns
the light on in the living room,

and finally welcomes you home.

Amphitrite

She is often swallowed
                    by whales
                              willingly.
          Between her breasts
                    peacock feathers.
               In her hair
                    many bright eyes.

               Her own belly harbors
                         a fish who has swallowed
                                        another fish.
She does not avoid
          inevitable pain,
                    but asks:
                         what need not be suffered?

A crane seems unperturbed
               he has grown
                         the tail of a squid
                                   and now swims
               beneath the water.

Perhaps for this reason,
                    she finds him
                              a welcome companion.

After Cancer Treatment

The language of this new country
is broken branches.

I am waiting
to hear them speak.

Having scraped together
what music they could

here on the windswept ridge,
they have come down

in a gravity of leaves.
Here is the solid ground

surviving the storm.
Here is the opened air,

the more and the less
of catastrophe, the nest

unhatched, the clogged
mouth of the burrow.

I've only old words
to call new things.

I walk the littered path
which says *kindling,*

which says *seed* and *sap.*

Donna Goes Dancing

When I want breasts, I wear my Dolly Parton bra.
Bigger than mine ever were—why not?
It's all make-believe now, like Dolly's hair.
My friend May wears her prosthesis every day,
but it makes her arm swell. When she goes home
she can't wait to take it off. I say, "May,
you've been through too much to keep helping people out.
If they don't know by now about cancer,
then it's time they did."
                                     She works at the courthouse,
says people stare. Or her kids say, "Mom
put it on—they'll think you're a freak."
I know she's got to do what she thinks right,
but it makes me mad when I see her hurting.

So when I went flat-footin' with Albert
I wore my Dolly boobs just for fun.
I was up on stage moving fast, my body
melting into lights and night air, the fiddle
racing up my spine, those boobs just thrashing
to get out, so I thought, Okay
this is for May.
                          I reached in my blouse
and grabbed one out, threw it to Albert
in the audience. He was surprised alright
but he laughed. That man's reflexes are good.
So I threw him the other. Watching those breasts
sail, nipples and all, over that many heads,
I felt like a girl again, glad to be
alive and dancing and free. I did it
for May—and for me.

Struck

My neighbor saw him jump
the fence in thunder,
leave the pasture for the road,
then back again, a flight
across boundaries as lightning
struck, and the rain came down,
as it does these days, urgent, torrential.

Struck by lightning, the oncologist said
that year I lost my breast to cancer
and I took to the neighborhood trails
as if I could walk off the earth itself,
walk through the valley of the shadow
into another country, walk because
my life depended on it, ceremony
of one foot in front of the other.

The tiny barn beside the road,
the hay, and no one, no one
that I saw, although a hidden hand
brought oats, the hay itself.
Each day he grazed the meager grass
of not-yet-spring, and we stepped,
one hoof, one foot, into the conversation
we'd neither of us had, as if horses and
humans had never spoken until we spoke.

He gave me a coltish welcome
once he knew I'd come most every afternoon,
any absence of that give-and-take, and a tug
of longing appeared, unaccountably, as if
a bond grew, more robust than was necessarily
wise. Or was it me so newly shorn of the other life
I wasn't sure how much love might break me?

We never thought saddles, but as if I
held the golden bridle, he came
of his own accord to the ritual of giving,
nosing my coat and pockets, twice nipping
the back of my hand when I withheld
what he knew I'd brought but was slow to give.
He taught me to offer an apple, not whole
but quartered and cored, no bitter seeds
between us. And then his muzzle
at my neck and ear.

Peg. We could say I was your gorgon,
and Perseus held the surgeon's knife,
but that's not how I'm telling the story.
And you, no thoroughbred, are safe
from our current Bellerophons who'd buy
you in quarters, pump you with steroids,
and race you so hard, so young
your forelegs would fracture
like the S through the staves
of a dollar sign.

Call me your Amazon, both of us
between worlds, those months
holding out, holding on,
apple a day before grass grew
green and lush and whoever thought
he owned you took you to another
field, but not before I dreamed you
crossed the threshold of my body,
saw what you saw, the winged
expanse, the fearsome flash.

How am I to know
if it was me leaving each day
by the same turning up the lane
as you watched, once even rushing
the fence as if you'd rather not part,
how am I to know if, when lightning
struck, you leapt toward more of what
we'd made, sanctuary
on the mountain, splitting the earth
open with one hoof, then another,
leaving not a feather behind
but green dung in the road
the sign of a living, breathing horse
who means to find me?

Bast

She finds pleasure in the body
of a cat. Ears swept up
to points, eyes tabby-lined,
she is arch and curve and stillness

one moment before motion.
Her ruff jewels into headdress,
veils shoulder and spine, falls to
emeralds on her furred breast.

Mau. The Egyptian word for cat,
cognate with mother. In what woman
is your origin? Related by blood.

Analogous in nature. She is what
must be abandoned

and cannot be relinquished,
that lush paradox:

batting paw, yawn,
twitched tail, purr.

After the Cave Paintings

Why do I stand unmoved,
jaded as a tabloid, refusing
astonishment, not down on
my knees, but sober as stone—
surely 19th-century spelunkers,
pranksters, or WWII resistance
fighters passing hours in the belly
of the mountain made these
bison, these bearded horses.

But carbon dating brings me
to my senses. Whatever I can't take
in—*1,500 generations, 32,000 years*—
here's human memory on the horns
of an ibex, our ancestors making it up
from scratch.
                    Is it all too near
to where I've been? Birth & Death.
Back and forth across that stuttering
line, illness a long darkness with only
a lantern and my love's strong
arm, the uneven, the unearthly
underfoot.
                    Stalactites make their own
sense of water and limestone
as I'm to make something wholly new
from the dripstone of another life.

Just as well we're not as firmly
anchored as we think.
In the thinned air, the wavering light,
easier to find that other self,
that knows as the animal
knows, as the bears in these caves
once knew, the first scratches on stone
their marks, beyond light, standing
upright on the old riverbed, so that
daughters of Adam, sons of Eve,
took up what the bears laid down,
dark claw on limestone, and drew.

Notes

The poems "Athena," "Amphitrite," "Eurydice," "Artemis," "Diana," "Astarte," "Bast," "Bird Goddess," and "Aphrodite," were inspired by Susan Seddon Boulet's *The Goddess Paintings* (San Francisco, CA: Pomegranate, 1994).

Raised in the nomadic subculture of the U.S. military, **KATHRYN KIRKPATRICK** was born in Columbia, South Carolina, and grew up in the Phillipines, Germany, Texas and the Carolinas. Today she lives with her husband, Will, and their two shelties in the Blue Ridge Mountains of North Carolina, and she currently holds a dual appointment at Appalachian State University as a Professor in the English Department and the Sustainable Development Program. She has a Ph.D. in Interdisciplinary Studies from Emory University, where she received an Academy of American Poets poetry prize. Her poetry collections include *The Body's Horizon* (1996), which was selected by Alicia Ostriker for the Brockman-Campbell award; *Beyond Reason* (2004), which was awarded the Roanoke-Chowan Poetry Prize by the North Carolina Literary and Historical Association; and *Out of the Garden* (2007), which was a finalist for the Southern Independent Booksellers Association poetry award. As a literary scholar in Irish studies and the environmental humanities, she has published essays on class trauma, ecofeminist poetics, and animal studies.